Getting To Know...

Nature's Children

LYNX

Merebeth Switzer

PUBLISHER	Joseph R. DeVarennes
PUBLICATION DIRECTOR	Kenneth H. Pearson
MANAGING EDITOR	Valerie Wyatt
SERIES ADVISOR	Merebeth Switzer
SERIES CONSULTANT	Michael Singleton
CONSULTANTS	Ross James
	Kay McKeever
	Dr. Audrey N. Tomera
ADVISORS	Roger Aubin
	Robert Furlonger
	Gaston Lavoie
EDITORIAL SUPERVISOR	Jocelyn Smyth
PRODUCTION MANAGER	Ernest Homewood
PRODUCTION ASSISTANTS	Penelope Moir
	Brock Piper

EDITORS

Katherine Farris   Anne Minguet-Patocka
Sandra Gulland   Sarah Reid
Cristel Kleitsch   Cathy Ripley
Elizabeth MacLeod   Eleanor Tourtel
Pamela Martin   Karin Velcheff

PHOTO EDITORS	Bill Ivy
	Don Markle
DESIGN	Annette Tatchell
CARTOGRAPHER	Jane Davie
PUBLICATION ADMINISTRATION	Kathy Kishimoto
	Monique Lemonnier

ARTISTS

Marianne Collins   Greg Ruhl
Pat Ivy   Mary Theberge

This series is approved and recommended by the Federation of Ontario Naturalists.

HU JP OK BB MD

Canadian Cataloguing in Publication Data

Switzer, Merebeth
  Lynx

(Getting to know—nature's children)
Includes index.
ISBN 0-7172-1909-7

1. Lynx—Juvenile literature.
I. Title. II. Series.

QL737.C23S97 1985   j599.74'428   C85-098718-0

Have you ever wondered . . .

if young lynx like to play? — page 6

who the lynx's nearest relatives are? — page 8

how to tell a lynx from a bobcat? — page 8

where lynx can be found? — page 11

how big a lynx is? — page 12

why the lynx has such big feet? — page 15

if a lynx ever gets cold feet? — page 15

how a lynx keeps cool in the summer? — page 16

what makes a lynx a successful hunter? — page 19

what lynx eat? — page 20

why a lynx climbs trees? — page 23

if a lynx has enemies? — page 23

how a lynx can hunt in the dark? — page 26

how a lynx marks its territory? — page 30

if all lynx have their own territory? — page 33

how a male lynx attracts a mate? — page 34

where a female lynx goes to have her babies? — page 38

what baby lynx look like? — page 41

how a mother lynx looks after her babies? — page 41

when lynx kittens start going outside? — page 41

how lynx kittens learn to hunt? — page 43

how a mother lynx cleans her kittens? — page 44

when young lynx leave home? — page 46

If you took a walk through the northern woods, you might be near a lynx without even knowing it. But you can be sure the lynx would know *you* were there. It might be peering out from under the low branches of an alder bush or looking down on you from its perch high in a spruce tree.

Lynx are the ghost cats of the northern woods. They are rarely seen, except at night, and as soon as they are spotted they disappear in a fast-moving blur.

Although there is something mysterious about the lynx, there is also something very familiar about it. Perhaps that is because it is a distant relative of our pet cats. Let's take a closer look at the lynx and see if we can discover more about this shy secretive cat.

It will come as no surprise that the lynx is a member of the cat family.

Playtime

Young lynx are a lot like kittens. In fact they are sometimes called kittens. And, like all young cats, they love to play. They leap out of the shadows at each other, tussle head over heels in the morning sunshine and then suddenly give up to swat a horsefly buzzing by. They scratch a nearby stump and then pounce, tumble, jump . . . they are back at the den where their mother is snoozing. After all that playing, the kittens are tired too. They nestle into their mother's soft silky fur for a quick catnap.

The Who's Who of Wild Cats

There are three wild cats in North America, the cougar, the bobcat and the lynx. The largest of the three is the cougar, also called the mountain lion or puma, and it is the easiest to recognize. It has a distinct sandy-brown coat and black muzzle, and it has a long tail.

You can tell the difference between the cougar's smaller relatives, the lynx and the bobcat, by looking at their tails. Both have short stumpy tails, but they have different markings. The lynx has a single, solid black tip on its tail. The bobcat's tail has a black tip too, but it has four or five dark rings around it and is somewhat longer.

You can also tell the lynx from the bobcat by its size, coat and ears. Generally, the lynx is larger, has longer legs and has fewer spots on its coat than the bobcat. It also has longer, far more distinctive tufts of fur on its ears.

Despite these differences, it is still a tricky business to tell these cats apart. Fortunately, the lynx and bobcat know who's who!

Lynx tail

Bobcat tail

Lynx Around the World

North American lynx have close cousins in Europe and Asia. Most lynx live in northern forest country. Some live still farther north, in the treeless tundra. But even these northerly lynx stay in shrub-covered areas where they can hide from enemies and avoid being seen by prey until the last possible moment.

Where lynx live in North America.

Lean and Lanky

The lynx has long legs and huge paws. This makes it seem to be a much larger animal than it really is. Actually, the lynx only weighs 8 to 11 kilograms (18-25 pounds), which is about the same as a one-year-old baby. Just think —if the lynx were willing, you could probably pick it up in your arms! As with most animals, the males are larger than the females.

In northern areas lynx may grow slightly bigger than their cousins who live more to the south.

A short black-tipped tail and snowshoe feet are the marks of a lynx.

Long-jumper Legs and Snowshoes

The lynx's long legs and over-sized paws are not just for appearances. They help it move quickly and easily, even in deep snow.

Thanks to its extra long legs, the lynx covers a great distance with each stride. Although it usually gallops along rather clumsily, it can move very quickly if it has to. Having powerful legs also means the lynx can leap gracefully over small thickets and fallen trees in the forest. In winter, the lynx's massive feet act like snowshoes. How? The furry toes spread far apart to distribute the lynx's weight out over the snow so that it does not sink in. Furry toes also help keep its feet warm. At temperatures of minus 35 degrees Celsius (minus 30 degrees Fahrenheit) warm feet are very important!

Although it has a husky build the lynx is very light on its feet.

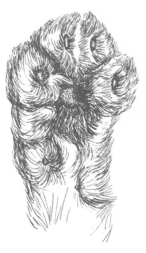

Hind paw

Front paw

15

Two Coats Are Better than One.

Because the lynx is active all year long, it needs two coats, a cool one for the summer and a warm one for winter.

The lynx's summer coat is quite short, but even so on hot days the lynx heads for a shady spot. There it lies down and sometimes even pants like a dog to cool down. This summer fur is light brown with faint spots. The brownish color and mottled pattern help the lynx blend into the shadows of the summer forest. In the fall, the lynx slowly sheds its summer fur. At the same time, a buffy gray winter coat with even fainter spots is growing in. The lynx's winter coat has two layers. The first layer is a dense underfur that works like a woolen blanket to keep in body warmth.

This underfur is covered by long, black-tipped guard hairs that protect the lynx from icy winds and shed water too. These sleek, silver-gray hairs are quite beautiful and very long. They can even be over 10 centimetres (4 inches) in length. That is longer than a new crayon!

Opposite page:

Few animals can boast a more beautiful and silky winter coat.

16

A Natural Hunter

Cats are some of the world's best equipped hunters, and the lynx is no exception. Its keen senses and strong, agile body, its powerful jaws and sharp teeth make it a very successful hunter indeed.

Just like a pet cat, the lynx sneaks up silently on its prey on its soft padded feet. It seems to know just where to step to make the least noise. It knows that even the snapping of a twig could cost it its dinner. If you have ever watched a house cat step gracefully around a row of houseplants or through a display of china ornaments, you have seen how a cat can do this.

When it is near its prey the lynx waits, and then quick as a flash, it bounds: one, two, three—success! The lynx will not be hungry tonight.

Ready to pounce.

The Hare Connection

The lynx hunts mice, voles, squirrels, grouse and even feeds on dead deer and caribou calves. But in winter, it depends mainly on Snowshoe Hares, which may make up three quarters or more of its diet.

Scientists have discovered that when there are only a few hares, there are only a few lynx. Then their numbers slowly begin to increase because each has plenty of food. The hares have lots of plants to munch on, and the lynx have lots of hares to hunt. But after about 10 years there are too many Snowshoe Hares for the amount of food available. So the number of hares begins to drop, and as it does, so too does the number of lynx. Then this 10-year cycle begins again . . .

Look Out Below!

The lynx is an excellent climber, and it often selects a tall tree for a lookout. From up in the tree it can spot prey without being seen.

It also climbs trees to escape if it is chased by a wolf. The lynx's climbing ability is less help, however, if its other main enemy, the cougar, is on its trail. A cougar can climb trees just as easily as the lynx. Like most cats, the lynx has a natural dread of the water. But it will do anything to escape a cougar—even swim!

On the prowl.

Night Senses

Because the lynx usually hunts at night it has extra-sensitive senses to help it find food. Its sense of smell is not very good but, like most cats, it can see well, even in the dark.

The next time you meet a cat, take a look at its special eyes. You will notice that the pupil, that black part in the center, changes size rapidly. In bright sunlight it is a tiny slit, but in the dark the pupil opens into a large dark circle. This allows more light to come into the eye so that the cat can see better. The lynx only sees in black and white and shades of gray. But even though it cannot see colors, it probably sees as well on a moonlit night as you do in broad daylight.

Lynx eye

Not accustomed to the bright daylight, this retiring lynx squints against the sun.

Whisker Warnings

The lynx does not rely totally on its eyes for hunting. It uses its shoulder-width face whiskers too. When the lynx is winding its way through thick underbrush or dark caves and the tips of its whiskers brush against something, it stops to size up the situation. Like other cats it knows that if its whiskers cannot fit through the rest of its body will not be able to squeeze through, either.

A lynx's whiskers are not there just for decoration. They are sensitive feelers that give the lynx important information.

Trespassers, Keep Out!

Male lynx have hunting territories which they defend against other males. How do lynx know whose territory belongs to whom? Each lynx marks his territory with special signs. To do this the male reaches high up on a tree trunk and scratches, sharpening his claws and leaving behind gouges in the wood. He then raises his hind leg and sprays the tree just as a dog does at a fire hydrant. This is known as a scent post or scrape, and it lets other lynx know: "This territory is taken. Stay out!"

Tree clawed by a lynx

The lynx is a loner.

These posts are marked regularly as the lynx makes a nightly tour over a wide network of trails. Down the river bank he pads, up a rocky slope, along a cliff ridge and across a deserted logging road. The lynx may travel as far as 19 kilometres (12 miles) each night marking his territory as he goes. If the scent on a scent post fades, a new lynx may chance moving into the territory.

The female lynx does not seem to be as concerned about claiming a special territory. Instead she is allowed to move in and out of the males' territories. Who knows—she might even prove to be a mate when mating season arrives! Although the male does not consider her a threat, the female lynx is by no means weak. She can and will fight a male challenger, especially when she has young to defend.

Love Songs

During the mating season, between January and March, the male lynx's love howls fill the night air. They attract females and challenge any other male who ventures into his territory. What a noisy ruckus! If you have ever heard a pair of tomcats yowling in your backyard, you can imagine the sound that echoes through the forest when two large male lynx are howling.

The drive to father the next generation is strong, and so two males often fight to see who will win a female. These catfights can be fierce. The two males spit and scream at each other. Soon they are a ball of flashing claws and flying fur. Who will win? Finally the weaker male leaves the fight before he receives any life-threatening injuries. He skulks off into the bush, leaving the stronger and healthier cat to be the father of the young. This helps to insure that the babies will be strong and healthy too.

The female is not far away and answers the victor's call with her own special yowls and purrs.

Opposite page:

You might find it hard to believe, but the yowls of this lovesick male are music to a female lynx's ears.

34

A Not-So-Dutiful Dad

Sometimes the male and the female lynx remain together for a few weeks to hunt and play. However, many males will leave their mate and look for yet another female to bear their young.

If the male lynx does stay with the female, she will drive him away long before the kittens are born. Male lynx are dangerous and have been known to kill their own kittens. Sometimes the male does not want to leave, but the female's hisses, bites and threats soon get the message across.

Mama Knows Best

Like many mothers, the lynx is very protective of her children. She keeps her kittens' birth and den a secret from the male and hidden from all of us too. But we do know some things about the lynx from studying the behavior of its close cousins.

The mother finds a secluded den, about two months after mating. Because she has to care for the kittens by herself, she needs a safe home with a good hunting ground nearby. After a search, she selects a site under the low branches of a spruce tree, inside a rotten log or in a dark dry cave.

Then the lynx gives birth to a litter of one to five kittens. When the tiny kittens are born, they are helpless gray balls of fluffy fur. They cannot see or hear, but within the next two weeks their eyes open and their hearing develops.

Lynx kittens are not helpless for long. Within two months they are sporting new coats and exploring the world.

Growing Up Fast

Although the baby lynx are only slightly larger than pet kittens, their large lynx paws are already big. For the first weeks they remain in the den and nurse on their mother's rich milk. Although the mother cat leaves them regularly to hunt for dinner, she is always nearby. She never knows when another lynx, or a cougar or wolf might find her babies, and she needs to be on hand to protect them.

Sometimes the mother lynx returns from her hunting trip with a special treat for her kittens—a juicy bone or a piece of meat. Gnawing on bones strengthens the kittens' jaws. And the occasional piece of meat gives them a taste of what they will hunt in the future.

By age two months, the kittens have lost the gray fluff they were born with. They now have rich red or buff-colored coats, dappled with soft brown spots. The curious young lynx kittens are everywhere. They play constantly . . . hide and seek, chase and pounce, tumble and tussle.

Opposite page:

The kittens stay with mom through their first winter.

41

Practice Makes Perfect

Playing prepares the kittens for one of the most important parts of their lives, hunting and catching their food. At two months they are not only sharing parts of their mother's meal, but they are ready to join her on her nightly hunts. The sooner they learn how to hunt, the better for all.

The female hides her young nearby while she stalks her prey, and the kittens learn by watching. Soon they are trying to catch their own dinner. They start with something small, a mouse or vole perhaps. And just as you probably do when you are learning something new, they make a lot of mistakes at first. But day by day their hunting skills improve.

Clean as a Whistle

The kittens grow rapidly, and by autumn they are almost as big as their mother. For the first time, they shed their summer fur, and a new thick winter coat grows in. Their long adult fur makes them look very much like their elegant parents.

A beautiful coat needs special care. For the past five months their mother has given them a thorough bath with her rough tongue to keep them clean. Now the young lynx must wash and groom their own fur. Combing and cleaning on a regular basis keeps the fur healthy, so it will keep them warm during the long winter.

Taking a catnap.

Family Farewells

The temperatures drop down lower and lower each fall night. The days get shorter and shorter. The first snows begin in the northern woods. The young lynx will stay with their mother through much of the winter.

In late winter or early spring the lynx family will split up. The mother does not want her young around when she mates, and, besides, the young are now able to look after themselves. The family will never be together again, but by next spring, the young lynx will be ready to start their own families.

Until then, each of these beautiful mysterious cats will prowl through the northern forests. They will suddenly leap out of nowhere and in an instant, they will be gone, vanishing like a secret silver shadow into the depths of the night.

Special Words

Den   Animal home.

Groom   To clean and brush.

Guard hairs   Long coarse hairs that make up the outer layer of the lynx's coat.

Mate   To come together to produce young. Either member of an animal pair is also the other's mate.

Mating season   The time of year during which animals mate.

Nurse   To drink the milk from a mother's body.

Prey   An animal hunted by another animal for food.

Pupil   The opening in the center of the eye which controls the amount of light taken in.

Scent post or **scrape**   Special signs that mark the boundaries of an animal's territory.

Territory   Area that an animal or group of animals lives in and often defends from other animals of the same kind.

INDEX

autumn, 44

babies. *See* kittens
bobcat, 8, 9

climbing, 23
coat, 9, 16, 38, 41, 44
communication, 34
cougar, 8, 23, 41

den, 6, 38, 41
diet, 20
distribution, 11

ears, 9
enemies, 23

family, 37, 46
female, 12, 33, 34, 37, 38, 41, 43

getting along, 30, 34
grooming, 44
growing up, 41, 43, 44
guard hairs, 15, 16

habitat, 5, 11, 15, 38
house cats, 5, 19, 41
hunting, 19, 20, 23, 26, 29, 30, 37, 43

kittens, 6, 37, 38, 41, 43, 44

legs, 12, 15
locomotion, 15

males, 12, 30, 33, 34, 37
mating season, 33, 34

night, 5, 26

paws, 12, 15, 19, 41
    illus. 15
playing, 6, 41, 43
population, 20
prey, 11, 19, 20, 23
pupil, 26

relatives, 8, 9

scratch marks, 30, 33
    illus. 30
scent posts, 30, 33
senses
    sight, 26, 29
    smell, 26
size, 9, 12
    of babies, 38, 41, 44
snow, 15
Snowshoe Hares, 20
summer, 16
swimming, 23

tail, 8
    illus. 9
teeth, 19
territory, 30, 33, 34

underfur, 16

whiskers, 29
winter, 16, 20, 44, 46
wolf, 23

Cover Photo: J.A. Wilkinson (Valan Photos)

Photo Credits: Tim Fitzharris (First Light Associated Photographers), pages 4, 10; T.W. Hall (Parks Canada), page 7; E. Schmidt (Valan Photos), pages 13, 24-25, 26, 28, 32, 42, 45; Wilf Schurig (Valan Photos), pages 14, 17; J.A. Wilkinson (Valan Photos), pages 18, 35; Michel Quintin (Valan Photos), page 21; Dennis Schmidt (Valan Photos), page 22; Stephen J. Krasemann (Valan Photos), page 31; National Film Board, page 37; E. Schmidecker (Miller Services), page 39; R. Spoenlein (Miller Services), page 40.

Getting To Know...

Nature's Children

SEA LIONS

Mark Shawver

PUBLISHER	Joseph R. DeVarennes	
PUBLICATION DIRECTOR	Kenneth H. Pearson	
MANAGING EDITOR	Valerie Wyatt	
SERIES ADVISOR	Merebeth Switzer	
SERIES CONSULTANT	Michael Singleton	
CONSULTANTS	Ross James	
	Kay McKeever	
	Dr. Audrey N. Tomera	
ADVISORS	Roger Aubin	
	Robert Furlonger	
	Gaston Lavoie	
EDITORIAL SUPERVISOR	Jocelyn Smyth	
PRODUCTION MANAGER	Ernest Homewood	
PRODUCTION ASSISTANTS	Penelope Moir	
	Brock Piper	
EDITORS	Katherine Farris	Anne Minguet-Patocka
	Sandra Gulland	Sarah Reid
	Cristel Kleitsch	Cathy Ripley
	Elizabeth MacLeod	Eleanor Tourtel
	Pamela Martin	Karin Velcheff
PHOTO EDITORS	Bill Ivy	
	Don Markle	
DESIGN	Annette Tatchell	
CARTOGRAPHER	Jane Davie	
PUBLICATION ADMINISTRATION	Kathy Kishimoto	
	Monique Lemonnier	
ARTISTS	Marianne Collins	Greg Ruhl
	Pat Ivy	Mary Theberge

This series is approved and recommended by the Federation of Ontario Naturalists.

Canadian Cataloguing in Publication Data

Shawver, Mark.
  Sea lion

(Getting to know—nature's children)
Includes index.
ISBN 0-7172-1934-8

1. Sea lions—Juvenile literature.
I. Title. II. Series.

QL737.P63S52 1985   j599.74'6   C85-098735-0

Have you ever wondered . . .

if a Sea Lion is a good mother?   page 7

what a baby Sea Lion is called?   page 7

who the Sea Lion's relatives are?   page 8

how to tell a Sea Lion from a seal?   page 11

where Sea Lions live?   page 12

how fast a Sea Lion can swim?   page 15

what Sea Lions use their hind flippers for?   page 16

what Sea Lions eat?   page 19

when Sea Lions eat?   page 19

how big Sea Lions are?   page 23

how Sea Lions keep warm?   page 24

how Sea Lions cool off?   page 24

why Sea Lions' eyes look so soft and gentle?   page 28

what a Sea Lion uses its whiskers for?   page 31

how a diving Sea Lion avoids a noseful of water?   page 32

what sounds Sea Lions make?   page 35

how many babies a mother Sea Lion has?   page 40

what a newborn Sea Lion looks like?   page 40

if Sea Lions have any enemies?   page 42

when baby Sea Lions start to swim?   page 45

if young Sea Lions like to play?   page 45

how long a young Sea Lion stays with its mother?   page 46

If you were to come upon a herd of Sea Lions, you would know it even before you saw them. They are noisy! As they lie about or frolic in the sun or clamber over each other on their way down to the ocean, they are never quiet and seldom still. A colony of Sea Lions is a busy place.

Unfortunately, the only Sea Lions most people see are trained ones in aquarium shows—the ones that balance balls on their noses, blow horns and clap their flippers on command. So let's look and see how these fascinating creatures—so clumsy on land, yet so graceful in the water—live in the wild.

Sea Lions come ashore to mate, breed and bask in the sun.

Puppy Love

Imagine yourself as a baby Sea Lion on a crowded beach where hundreds of Sea Lions have gathered. The world is still very new and you have much to learn. Suddenly, you hear the thunderous growling of two enormous Sea Lions fighting each other. You look up and see that one of them has been given a huge shove and is rolling your way. You are certain to be crushed! But at the last second, you are grabbed by the neck and yanked away to safety. Although you were unaware of it, your mother has been watching over you and has come to your rescue.

Scenes like this happen quite often. For the first five or six months of a Sea Lion's life, its mother is nearby, ready to protect it. Mother and baby spend much of their time lying on the beach, snuggling close together. The little one, called a pup, especially enjoys stretching out on its mother's back for an afternoon nap.

This Sea Lion pup is looking for its mother.

Fin-Footed

Sea Lions belong to a group of animals called pinnipeds. The word *pinniped* means "fin-footed." They were given this name because their feet are effective swimming fins.

Pinnipeds can be divided into three groups. Sea Lions and their close cousins, the Fur Seals, are called eared seals. All other seals are called earless seals. Both kinds of seals are related to the third kind of pinniped, the walrus.

*Sea Lion
front flipper*

*Sea Lion
back flipper*

Sea Lions "haul out" onto rocky shores to rest.

Seal or Sea Lion?

What is the difference between a Sea Lion and most seals? The easiest way to tell is to compare their ears and the way they walk. If the animal has no visible ear flaps and crawls on the land on its stomach like a big caterpillar, it is a seal. If it has small ears on the side of its head and walks on its four flippers, it is a Sea Lion or a Fur Seal.

There are two kinds of Sea Lions along the coast of North America—the Northern Sea Lion and the more common California Sea Lion.

Sea Lions have tiny ear flaps on both sides of their head.

Where They Live

In North America, Sea Lions can be found on the West Coast from the cold waters of Alaska's Bering Sea to the warm tropical waters off California and Mexico. Northern Sea Lions prefer rocky shores, while California Sea Lions like sand or boulder beaches backed by cliffs.

During the fall and winter, the males travel great distances in search of better fishing areas. The females usually stay fairly close to the breeding grounds, teaching their pups how to take care of themselves.

Northern Sea Lion

California Sea Lion

Super Swimmers

A Sea Lion is certainly at its best in the water. Every movement is graceful as it spins and twirls in an underwater ballet. Several thrusts of its flippers can send the Sea Lion gliding through the water at speeds of about 24 to 32 kilometres (15 to 20 miles) per hour.

The Sea Lion has large paddle-like front flippers that are about as long as a man's arm. These flippers flap up and down much like the wings of a bird.

Sea Lions can't breathe underwater so they must surface for air.

The shorter hind flippers are used to steer the animal in the water. On land the hind flippers bend forward and are used for walking.

Sea Lions are great divers and enjoy diving from rocks or boulders at the water's edge. But they must be very careful not to be thrown against the rocks by the crashing waves.

The Sea Lion's streamlined, torpedo-shaped body helps it to be one of nature's best swimmers. Its body glides almost effortlessly through the water.

For getting around on land, the Sea Lion uses all four flippers.

A Fishy Feast

Sea Lions get all of their food from the ocean. They enjoy meals of herring and other kinds of fish, such as cod, flounder and greenling. They also eat squid and octopus.

Sea Lions mostly feed at night. They must move quickly to catch their slippery meals. They capture the prey and hold it tightly in their powerful jaws. They rarely chew their food. Instead they swallow it whole. If the fish is too big to be swallowed in one gulp, the Sea Lion shakes it vigorously to break it into bite-sized pieces.

Usually Sea Lions hunt by themselves or with a few companions. But when a school of herring swims by, many Sea Lions will join in the hunt. Even Sea Lions enjoying an afternoon nap wake up to take part in the fishy feast.

Sometimes a Sea Lion will chase a fish just for the fun of it. It will catch it, let it go, chase it around some more and then let it go again. Sea Lions seem to enjoy this game!

Heavy Weights

Do you know that some Sea Lions may grow to be the size of a small car? In fact, the Northern Sea Lion may weigh up to 900 kilograms (2000 pounds) and reach a length of about three metres (9 feet). The average California Sea Lion, however, is much smaller. It weighs about 250 kilograms (550 pounds) and measures about two and a half metres (8 feet) long. The females are only about one-third the weight of the males.

The male, or bull, Sea Lions are usually brown in color. The females, or cows, are a lighter shade of brown. But when their fur gets wet, Sea Lions look almost black.

Northern Sea Lions may start life tiny, but some grow to be larger than a Polar Bear.

Cozy Warm

The Sea Lion has several ways of staying cozy warm even in chilly waters. A thick layer of fat, called blubber, lies under the Sea Lion's skin. This blubber layer keeps the Sea Lion's body heat in and the cold out.

The Sea Lion has another way of keeping warm, too. It grows a thick coat of fur. The hairs grow so close together that water never gets right down to the skin. Millions of tiny air bubbles trapped in the thick fur also help keep the cold out and the heat in.

In summer, Sea Lions can get too warm. To cool off, they may jump into the water. Sometimes they pant like dogs or wave their flippers in the air like fans. The flippers do not have blubber, so heat from the Sea Lion's body can escape through them.

A fur coat is not a luxury for a Sea Lion. In these icy waters it is a necessity!

New Coats for Old

After a whole year of climbing on rocks, lying on rugged beaches and fighting and playing, a Sea Lion's fur coat becomes very ragged looking. This ragged fur no longer keeps the Sea Lion as warm as it once did. So, each spring when the Sea Lions are on the beaches, their old fur falls out and new fur grows in. Because they are not in the water much at this time of year, missing some of their fur for a few weeks does not seem to bother them. When this process, called molting, is finished the Sea Lion sports a brand-new, shiny coat of fur.

Loafing in the sun.

Underwater Eyes

If you were to dive deep into the ocean, you probably would have trouble seeing. This is because it is dark and murky, and human eyes are not suited to seeing in these conditions. A Sea Lion has large brown eyes with pupils that open up wide to let in more light. This helps it see in the shadowy depths where humans cannot.

As well, Sea Lions have a clear, protective layer that covers their open eyes to protect them when underwater. This layer is what gives a Sea Lion's eyes their soft, gentle look. They also have eyelids much like our own that protect their eyes while on land. And, like us they close their eyes when they sleep.

On land, the Sea Lion's eyes are also protected by tears that help carry away sand or dirt. The tears flow freely down their cheeks, making it seem that Sea Lions are always crying.

Few animals are as graceful in the water as a Sea Lion.

"Seeing" in the Dark

If someone turned out the light, how would you find your way around? You would probably use your hands to feel your way. The night-feeding Sea Lion is often in the dark when it hunts for fish underwater. But, instead of using hands, it feels its way around with the help of its whiskers.

The whiskers are controlled by tiny muscles and are used much like we use our fingers to explore our surroundings. They are equipped with sensitive nerves. Using them, a Sea Lion can tell a slippery octopus from a piece of wood. A trained Sea Lion can even use its whiskers to help balance a ball on the tip of its nose.

The Sea Lion's sensitive whiskers are an important part of its fishing gear.

Other Senses

The Sea Lion is able to close its nostrils so that it does not get a noseful of water when it dives. It does have a keen sense of smell, however. In fact, a mother can tell her pup from all others just by sniffing it.

Sea Lions can hear sounds underwater just as well as they do on land. They have short tube-like ears about the size of your little toe, and they cock their outer ear flaps much the way a dog does to focus in-coming sounds.

A Sea Lion's sense of smell is only useful on land. While underwater its nostrils are closed.

Sea Dogs . . .

Sea Lions are very noisy animals, especially when they are gathered together on a beach. They make an UHH, UHH sound, growl and sometimes even bark. In fact, old-time sailors used to call them sea dogs.

The bark can mean several things. A bull will bark loudly to let other males know to stay away from his territory. The barking sound can also help a mother find a missing pup. She is able to tell her own infant's barking bleat from all the others, even though hundreds of pups may be barking at the same time.

Barking is also used as a warning signal. When danger is near, the bull starts to bark rapidly and run toward the sea. He will soon be followed by other Sea Lions. Sea Lions also bark underwater. This barking can be heard for long distances.

When a Sea Lion has something to say it believes in saying it—loud and clear.

And Sea Lions

You may have wondered why we call these huge un-lion-like animals Sea Lions. All you have to do is hear a Northern Sea Lion roar and you will instantly know why. If you closed your eyes you might think you were in the jungle hearing a lion roar.

Big Bullies

In the spring, with the coming of warmer weather and longer days, Sea Lions begin to gather on beaches to give birth and to mate. The place where they gather is called a rookery.

Among California Sea Lions, the bulls arrive at the rookery first to claim an area of beach for themselves. This is their territory, and it is where their pups will be born. The females arrive later and settle in a bull's territory. In good territories, there may be 15 or more females. Among Northern Sea Lions, the females arrive first, followed by the bulls.

The group of females in one bull's territory is called a harem. The bull defends his territory by chasing off intruders. Very rarely do the bulls fight, but there is always a lot of barking and growling going on!

The males and females that are too young or too old to mate usually stay on the outskirts of the rookery. If they try to venture in, they will be chased away by one "big bully" after another.

Opposite page:

Northern Sea Lion colony.

Life on the Beach

Sea Lions mate in the summer while on the beaches and the female gives birth to a single pup the following year.

The newborn does not have a cozy nursery as some animals do. Instead, it is born right on the beach among hundreds of other Sea Lions.

The little one looks much like its mother, except that it is smaller and darker. The pup is about 85 to 100 centimetres (33-39 inches) long and weighs about 16 kilograms (35 pounds). Its eyes are wide open and it has a nice shiny coat of fur.

Within a few hours of its birth, the pup begins to drink its mother's milk. Because this milk is so rich, the pup grows very quickly. Although it will nurse for almost a year, it will start eating fish at about six months.

The bull spends most of its time patrolling its territory and pays very little attention to the newborn pups.

Opposite page:

Young Sea Lions cannot yet roar or even bark. Instead they bleat like young lambs.

40

On the Lookout

Sea Lions have little to fear as they swim, hunt and play in the ocean. However, there are two enemies that the Sea Lion is always on the lookout for. Can you guess who they are?

It is no surprise that one is the shark and the other is the Killer Whale. In a fight with either of these two animals, even the largest of Sea Lions is almost defenseless. Its only chance is to swim quickly or turn quickly to avoid the attacker.

If the Sea Lion can hide in a bed of underwater seaweed or make it to the beach, it may be safe. However, it must still be alert since Killer Whales sometimes slide a little way onto the shore to try to grab an unsuspecting Sea Lion.

Usually, the Sea Lion's enemies take the sick or weak animals which are unable to swim fast enough to get away. Mother Sea Lions must be very watchful to protect their pups.

Mom and her pup should be safe here. The water is too shallow for a shark or a Killer Whale.

Swimming Lessons

How old were you when you took your first swimming lesson? Older than a Sea Lion for sure: a Sea Lion starts swimming when it is only about ten days old. The pup follows its mother to a tidepool, where the water is shallow and calm. They play together, close to the shore. If the pup gets tired, it will often climb up onto its mother's back for a rest.

The pup soon becomes skillful in twisting and turning in the water. This is very important because the next lesson is how to catch a fish! The pup has to learn when to breathe so it will not take water into its lungs. When the mother has had enough playtime, she often carries the pup out of the water in her mouth.

After several weeks in the tidepool and shallows, the pup is ready for the deeper water, farther from shore. It quickly learns to dive below the crashing waves, closing its nose to keep the water out.

Opposite page:

Sea Lion pups stay close to mother's side for the first two weeks of their lives.

Challenges of the Deep

Young Sea Lions are very playful. They toss pebbles back and forth and chase each other around in the water with many leaps and dives. They even play hide and seek in the underwater forest of kelp and seaweed.

Since the layer of blubber that keeps it warm is very thin, the pup can spend only short periods of time in the water. As the pup gets older, the blubber layer grows thicker, allowing it to stay warm on longer swims.

By four months of age, most young Sea Lions are expert swimmers and can stay underwater for about seven minutes. By six months, the pup is ready to swim and hunt for fish on its own, although it stays close to its mother until the following spring. Then it will take its place on the outskirts of the rookery until it is ready to start a family of its own. In the wild, Sea Lions can live to be up to 17 years old and have many pups.

Special Words

Blubber   A thick layer of fat just below the skin.

Bull   A male Sea Lion.

Cow   A female Sea Lion.

Harem   A group of females in a bull's territory.

Kelp   A type of underwater plant, like seaweed.

Mate   To come together to produce young.

Molting   When an animal loses its fur and it is replaced with new fur.

Nurse   To drink milk from the mother's body.

Pinnipeds   A group of animals whose legs are specially shaped as flippers. Seals, Sea Lions and walruses are pinnipeds.

Pupil   The part of the eye that gets larger or smaller depending on the amount of light.

Territory   An area on the beach that a bull claims to be his own.

Tidepool   A small pool of water on the beach.

Rookery   An area on shore where Sea Lions go to mate, give birth and raise their young.

INDEX

babies. *See* pups
barking, 5, 35, 36
blubber, 24, 46
breathing, 45
breeding grounds, 12
bulls, 12, 23, 39, 40

California Sea Lion, 11, 12, 23, 39
coat, 24, 27, 40
colony, 5, 7, 39, 40
color, 23, 40
cows, 12, 23, 39, 40, 42, 45, 46

diet, 19
  of pups, 40
distribution, 12
diving, 16, 28

eared seals, 8
earless seals, 8
ears, 11, 32
eating habits, 19
enemies, 42
eyes, 28

females. *See* cows
fighting, 7, 27, 39
fishing, 12, 19, 45
flippers, 5, 8, 11, 15, 16, 24
Fur Seals, 8

habitat, 12, 39
harem, 39

males. *See* bulls
mating, 40
molting, 27

Northern Sea Lion, 11, 12, 23, 36, 39

pinnipeds, 8
playing, 19, 45, 46
pups, 7, 12, 39, 40, 42, 45, 46

rookery, 39

sense of smell, 32

size, 23
  of pups, 40
speed, 15
staying cool, 24
staying warm, 24
steering, 16
swimming, 15, 16, 19, 28, 42, 45, 46

tears, 28
territory, 39, 40
tidepool, 45
trained Sea Lions, 5, 31

walking, 8, 11, 16
walrus, 8
whiskers, 31

Cover Photo: Herman Giethoorn (Valan Photos)

Photo Credits: Barry Ranford, pages 4, 13, 33; Peter Thomas (Image Finders Photo Agency), pages 6, 23; Herman Giethoorn (Valan Photos), pages 9, 29, 43; Network Stock Photo File, page 10; Tim Fitzharris (First Light Associated Photographers), pages 14, 25, 34; Bruno Kern, pages 17, 26; Don Herrigan (Master File), pages 18; Hälle Flygare (Valan Photos), pages 20-21; J.D. Taylor (Miller Services), pages 30, 44; Wayne Lynch (Master File), pages 36-37, 41; John Foster (Master File), page 38.